GOD'S FIRE FOR ELIJAH

1 Kings 18:16–39 for children
Written by Giles Zimmer • Illustrated by Allan Eitzen

CONCORDIA PUBLISHING HOUSE • SAINT LOUIS

Elijah was a man of God.
He tried hard to be good.
Elijah only prayed to God
As every person should.

Now Ahab was a wicked king.
He always prayed to Baal.
Elijah told him this was bad,
That he was sure to fail.

Elijah said to Ahab,
"I'll prove it now to you.
High up on the mountain,
I'll prove my God is true."

So all the priests who prayed to Baal,
The common people too,
Climbed up upon the mountain
To see what he would do.

Elijah said to all of them,
"Be careful whom you praise.
If you are bringing gifts to Baal,
You've got to change your ways.

"I'll show you that my God is true,
And not that awful Baal.
The god of all these wicked priests
Is feeble and is frail."

"The priests will offer up a bull,
And I will do the same.
And then the God who's really true
Will send down heaven's flame."

The priests began to pray to Baal.
They yelled and beat the air.
They jumped and danced till it was noon
And offered Baal their prayer.

Elijah laughed until he hurt
To see them dance and sweat.
He egged them on and jeered at them
Till they were dripping wet.

"Now where's your god you think is true?
Has he gone out to eat?
Perhaps he stopped along the road.
He's sleeping in the heat."

They cut their arms and legs with knives
And made a frightful din.
No fire came from heaven though.
Baal could never win!

Elijah dug a ditch around
His altar and the bull.
He had the people water it.
The ditch was running full.

He made them water it some more.
"Go flood that ditch," he cried.
The altar never would be lit
No matter what they tried.

He made them do it once again.
"Now everything is set
For God to burn my sacrifice,
Even though it's wet."

Elijah prayed to God that day,
"Lord, show what You can do."
And fire fell from up above
And proved that God was true.

All the wicked priests of Baal
Scampered off like mice,
When they saw the fire from God
Burn up the sacrifice!

Dear Parents:

With conviction and absolute faith Elijah confronts King Ahab and declares that there is only one true God. In a truly miraculous way God proves this point as He brings fire down upon the sacrifice of Elijah even though it has been drenched with water. What a spectacular sight that must have been!

Children today are impressed by sensational sights and dramatic special effects. Help your child to realize that this miracle was even more spectacular than the most sensational special effect because it happened through God's power and God's power alone. Review the many miracles that show the power of God. Remind your child that the greatest show of God's power was the victory over sin, death, and Satan that was won through the death and resurrection of His Son, our Savior, Jesus Christ.

The Editor